a line around england

simon harmer

a line around england

a colouring book of the nation's favourite landmarks

PORTICO

For my mother, Diana Harmer

First published in the United Kingdom in 2015 by
Portico
1 Gower Street
London WC1E 6HD
An imprint of Pavilion Books Company Ltd

ISBN 9781909881228

A CIP catalogue record for this book is available
from the British Library.

20 19 18 17 16 15
10 9 8 7 6 5 4 3 2 1

Reproduction by Mission Productions Ltd, Hong Kong
Printed and bound by 1010 Printing International Ltd,
China

This book can be ordered direct from the publisher
at the website www.pavilionbooks.com, or try your
local bookshop.

contents

The illustrations are arranged to form a linear journey through England, starting in the north at Hadrian's Wall and moving in a southerly direction towards the Cornish coast. They are listed alphabetically here for ease of reference.

Introduction	8
Angel of the North	14
Bath's Roman Baths	94
Battersea Power Station	54
Blackpool Tower	28
Bodiam Castle	76
Brighton Pier	78
Brownsea Island	86
Buckingham Palace	52
Canterbury Cathedral	72
Chartwell	68
Chatsworth	34
Cheddar Gorge	98
Clifton Suspension Bridge	100

Corfe Castle	88
Cornish Mines & Engines	108
Durham Cathedral	16
The Eden Project	104
Fountains Abbey & Studley Royal Water Gardens	24
Greenway	102
Hadrian's Wall	12
Hampton Court Palace	50
Hill Top	20
Houses of Parliament	56
Lake District	18
Liver Building	30
Leeds Castle	70
London Eye	58

Maunsell Forts 66

The Needles 84

The O$_2$ 64

Peak District 36

Quarry Bank Mill 32

St Michael's Mount 106

Salisbury Cathedral 90

Shakespeare's House 40

Spinnaker Tower 82

Stonehenge 92

Stourhead 96

Tintagel 110

Tower Bridge 62

Tower of London 60

Uffington White Horse 44

Waddesdon Manor 42

Wenlock Edge 38

Wembley Stadium 48

White Cliffs of Dover 74

Windsor Castle 46

Winchester Cathedral 80

York Minster 26

Yorkshire Dales 22

Acknowledgements 112

introduction

England has a wealth of history and culture that has
fascinated me since I was a child. I have always marvelled
at the huge diversity that this amazing country has to offer –
from ancient ruins, through to areas of outstanding natural
beauty, and modern masterpieces of design and architecture.

I grew up in Shropshire, a county full of rolling arable
landscapes, with the mighty Severn River snaking its way
towards the coast at Bristol. I was inspired by the historical
architecture around me, in my home town of Shrewsbury.
After graduating from Portsmouth University, where I fell

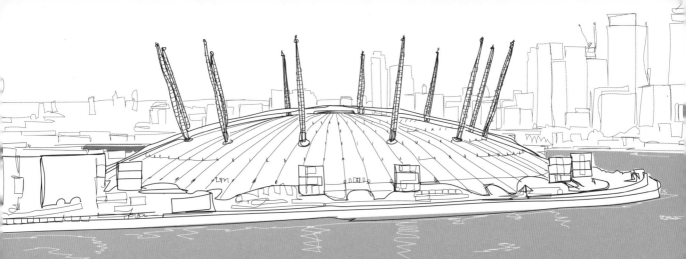

in love with the coastal landscape, I settled in Winchester and began drawing all I saw around me – a wealth of ancient monuments and historical buildings. Casting my eye further, I looked at Salisbury and its imposing cathedral, as well as our most iconic of monuments, Stonehenge.

It became clear to me that there was a visual story running across the entire country, from north to south, east to west, and that it might be possible to capture some of this in one piece of work. The challenge was not so much what to include in the book, but what could be omitted. The scope for a book like this is huge – so many cathedrals, monuments, castles and grand houses from our incredible history. Huge areas of stunning natural beauty – National Parks, rivers, lakes and hundreds of miles of incredible coastline.

This book is my tribute to this amazing country, and all that it has to offer. It is a collection of fifty illustrations – a linear journey from Hadrian's Wall in the North, through the industrial North West, the Lake and Peak Districts, down through London, the home counties, Hampshire and across to the South West and Cornwall. Each illustration is a key landmark, historic or architectural, with an accompanying piece about its history and importance.

I have approached each landmark as a separate work of art, one which can hopefully be admired for its own beauty and importance. Similarly, there is a continuity throughout the book which ties the journey together, both in terms of style and location. Some of the pieces have a personal resonance for me, either from childhood or as places that I connect with from

an aesthetic point of view. Some are simply beautiful to draw,
others are icons that simply could not be left out. Each drawing
is an almost continuous line, travelling across the page much
as your eye would take in a scene. A simple splash of colour
is added to lift the illustration, giving emphasis and depth.

I hope you will enjoy the journey as much as I have enjoyed
creating it. You will have your favourites, as I do, and I'm sure
the book will open up the possibility of new experiences, or
share some knowledge with you that was previously unknown.
If nothing else, it will share with you my love for drawing, for
creating something to be enjoyed by others, and reinforce the
beauty and variety of everything that England has to offer.

hadrian's wall
cumbria & northumberland

Emperor Hadrian ordered the building of the wall in AD 122, 'to separate the Romans from the barbarians'. Built using materials close to hand, the wall has different sections, from huge stones to simple turf. Construction took only six years, which is an achievement considering the hilly terrain the wall crosses. In places it reaches some 3m (10ft) wide and 6m (20ft) high; it also includes fortifications.

This impressive defensive wall (now a UNESCO World Heritage Site) spans some 129km (80 miles) across northern England, from the Solway Firth in Cumbria to Wallsend in Tyne & Wear, crossing the Pennines en route.

The route is now a national walking trail and along the way you can explore the wall's rich history in the Roman forts of Birdoswald, Vindolanda, Housesteads and Chesters; nearby are the ruins of the Roman garrison town of Corbridge.

angel of the north
tyne & wear

This immense steel sculpture by Antony Gormley is perched on a hill overlooking the A1 in Gateshead, Tyne & Wear.

Gormley says of his sculpture: 'When you think of the mining that was done underneath the site, there is a poetic resonance. Men worked beneath the surface in the dark. Now in the light, there is a celebration of this industry.'

The angel weighs 200 tonnes, stands over 20m (66ft) high, and its wings span a colossal 54m (177ft). The sculpture was erected in 1998 and it is estimated that it is seen by around 33 million people a year, due in the most part to its proximity to main transport routes in and out of Newcastle.

durham cathedral
durham

This amazing Norman cathedral was built to house
the shrine of St Cuthbert, and to provide a residence for
Benedictine monks in 1093. It is also home to the tomb
of the Venerable Bede. The nave is 143m (469ft) in length,
and its central tower reaches a height of 66m (217ft), giving
stunning views over Durham. It has been a focal point in
the north-east of England for centuries.

In addition to the architectural treasures of the cathedral,
visitors can climb the tower, and wander the cloister and
undercroft. In 1986 it was inscribed on the World Heritage
list by UNESCO, as part of the Durham World Heritage Site.

lake district
cumbria

One of England's largest and most beautiful national parks, the Lake District occupies an area of roughly 2,292 sq. km (885 sq. miles) in Cumbria. The sixteen largest and most well-known lakes, and the many tarns, nestle among dramatic mountains, crags and fells. It contains England's highest mountain (Scafell Pike) and deepest lake (Wastwater).

The area is synonymous with many famous authors and artists, from William Wordsworth and John Ruskin to Beatrix Potter and Alfred Wainwright, who have been inspired by the beauty of the landscape. Beatrix Potter in particular was instrumental in the preservation of the land, and her bequest of over 16 sq. km (4000 acres) and 14 farms to the National Trust has helped to keep the area relatively unspoilt.

hill top
cumbria

Hill Top, near Hawkshead in Cumbria, was home to Beatrix
Potter and is now looked after by the National Trust.

In 1905, following the success of her first book, *Peter Rabbit*,
and subsequent books in the series, Beatrix Potter was able
to buy this seventeenth-century farmhouse and make
it her home. She continued to write many more books,
taking inspiration from her house and garden.

When bequeathing the house and surrounding land to the
National Trust, Beatrix Potter stipulated how they should be
arranged and managed after her death. The National Trust
has kept it as she intended since taking over management
of the estate in 1946, and the cottage garden continues to
thrive with many heritage varieties of flowers and fruits.

yorkshire dales
yorkshire

The Yorkshire Dales is an Area of Outstanding Natural Beauty situated in North Yorkshire. The area broadly known as the Dales covers nearly 1,800 sq. km (695 sq. miles), and part of it is designated as a national park.

Tourists come from far and wide to enjoy the breathtaking beauty of the Dales, from its towering limestone cliffs at Malham Cove to its quaint riverside towns such as Burnsall (shown opposite). Straddling the Pennines, the area is also well known for its cave systems and waterfalls such as Hardraw Force, which has a reputed drop of 30m (100ft).

Despite the number of tourists who flock to the Dales, it remains a place of vast unspoilt wilderness and invokes a true sense of solitude and tranquility.

fountains abbey &
studley royal water gardens
yorkshire

Just outside Ripon in North Yorkshire stands the remains of magnificent Fountains Abbey. This Grade I listed building is part of a UNESCO World Heritage Site and is nearly 900 years old, having been founded in 1132.

The abbey buildings were in use right up until 1539, when Henry VIII ordered the dissolution of the monasteries. At this time it was considered to be the richest Cistercian abbey in the country.

Fountains Abbey remains the largest monastic ruin in England. Today the ruins are open to visitors, as part of a wider estate including Studley Royal Water Gardens, all looked after by the National Trust.

york minster
york

The Cathedral and Metropolitical Church of St Peter in York – the Minster's formal title – dates back to 627, and the current Gothic cathedral was built between 1220 and 1472. It is the seat of the Archbishop of York, the cathedral of the diocese of York, and one of the finest and largest buildings of its kind in northern Europe.

York Minster contains some incredible architecture, including the largest expanse of medieval stained glass in the world in its Great East Window. Local legend states that couples who kiss under the 'Heart of Yorkshire' window will stay together forever.

The cathedral – which has endured fires, Viking invasion and lightning strikes – is an iconic site in North Yorkshire, attracting thousands of visitors every year.

blackpool tower
blackpool

In the late nineteenth century, the mayor of Blackpool, Sir John Bickerstaffe, visited Paris and decided that Blackpool should have its own Eiffel Tower. In 1894 the tower opened to the public, stretching some 158m (518ft) into the Lancashire skyline.

The Grade I listed tower is not only an icon of architectural significance; for me it also evokes memories of the archetypal English seaside towns of the past, casting its huge shadow over the beach where donkey rides can still be enjoyed.

The tower has also long been a home of entertainment, with its famous ballroom hosting many spectacular dance events. Since 1894, the Tower Circus has also been in operation, not missing a single season in all that time. Other attractions have included a menagerie and aquarium, a large indoor children's play area, the Tower Dungeon, and the terrifying Walk of Faith – a glass panel at the top of the tower upon which visitors can stroll (if they have a head for heights!) and see the town spread under their feet.

liver building
liverpool

Once the tallest building in the UK, Liverpool's Royal Liver Building was purpose-built as the headquarters for the Royal Liver Friendly Society. Begun in 1908, the building was completed in 1911 and stands some 98m (322ft) high, with two iconic birds (the Liver Birds) – each standing 5.5m (18ft) tall – perched on top of the two towers.

The birds face in opposite directions: one to the city and one to the sea. It is said that if the two birds were to fly away, the Merseyside city would 'cease to exist'.

Now a Grade I listed building, the landmark also forms part of the UNESCO-designated World Heritage Maritime Mercantile City.

quarry bank mill
cheshire

Now a museum, this immense textile mill in Styal, Cheshire, is a reminder of England's industrial heritage. Built in 1784, the mill houses Europe's most powerful working waterwheel and was founded by the Greg family, who employed hundreds of local people to work on the site.

To house the growing workforce, Samuel Greg expanded the nearby Styal village. He carefully planned the village to ensure a better way of life for his workers, which included setting up a school for the local children.

The mill continued in production right up until 1959, having been donated to the National Trust in 1939. It remains a popular heritage site; every year over 150,000 visitors learn how the mill workers and machinery produced cotton.

chatsworth
derbyshire

My abiding memory of this amazing stately home is as the fictional house of Mr Darcy, in the 2005 film adaption of Jane Austen's *Pride and Prejudice*. The reality is that this famous jewel, near Bakewell in the Derbyshire countryside, is the long-time seat of the Duke of Devonshire, and has been home to sixteen generations of the Cavendish family since 1549.

There is plenty for visitors to take in: the magnificent house and a significant art collection, as well as the park, gardens and farm; the estate also hosts many events.

peak district
derbyshire

Home to Britain's first national park, the Peak District is a spectacular area of beautiful countryside covering 1,437 sq. km (555 sq. miles) across much of Derbyshire in northern England.

Every year millions of people flock to see its stunning views, and although the Peak District's name suggests a landscape of dramatic mountains, the dominant features are rolling hills, farmland and moorland. At points, it neighbours large cities including Manchester, Huddersfield and Sheffield.

Accessible from many locations and home to many charming villages, the park has much to offer visitors. Hiking and walking are popular pastimes, as is tasting the famous Bakewell pudding from the town of the same name.

wenlock edge
shropshire

Growing up in Shropshire, Wenlock Edge was a part of my childhood, not least because of the legends that surround this amazing limestone escarpment. Situated near Much Wenlock, it stretches approximately 30km (19 miles) across the Shropshire countryside. Now a Site of Special Scientific Interest (SSSI), it was formed by a coral reef millions of years ago and provides spectacular views.

During the English Civil War in 1642–49, Major Thomas Smallman fled from his nearby home at Wilderhope Manor. Trapped by Roundhead soldiers, and carrying important documents, he rode his horse over the edge, falling over 60m (197ft). Although the horse died, Smallman survived, carrying his dispatches to Shrewsbury. It is thought that his ghost and that of his horse still roam the area.

Another piece of local folklore refers to a fearsome bandit named Ippikin, who buried his treasure nearby. If you were to stand on the escarpment and say: 'Ippikin, Ippikin, keep away with your long chin', legend has it you will be pushed over the edge by the robber's ghost.

shakespeare's house
warwickshire

Situated in the heart of Stratford-upon-Avon in Warwickshire, this is the house in which the world's most famous playwright, William Shakespeare, was born and raised.

The house on Henley Street is thought to date from the mid-sixteenth century and features a large oak frame and, typical of the period, a wattle-and-daub construction. It was originally part of a terrace of similar houses, which were demolished as part of the restoration of the house in order to prevent any potential fires spreading.

Today the house is a museum, with the modern Shakespeare Centre now attached. Both buildings are owned and managed by the Shakespeare Birthplace Trust, which bought the house when it was sold by the Hart family, descendants of Shakespeare, in 1847.

waddesdon manor
buckinghamshire

Waddesdon Manor was built by Baron Ferdinand de Rothschild in 1874, in the style of a French Renaissance chateau. It nestles in the Oxfordshire countryside, just six miles from Aylesbury.

The house remained in the family until 1957, when James de Rothschild bequeathed the house to the National Trust. It has become one of the Trust's most popular attractions, with over 385,000 visitors per year.

When it was built, the house was a pinnacle of modern luxury, with a steel frame, central heating, hot and cold water and an electric bell system. The house is also famous for its stunning gardens, beautifully designed by the French landscape architect Elie Lainé. Visitors can marvel at the newly renovated aviary, as well as the coach house and stables converted into a gallery for an exhibition of contemporary art.

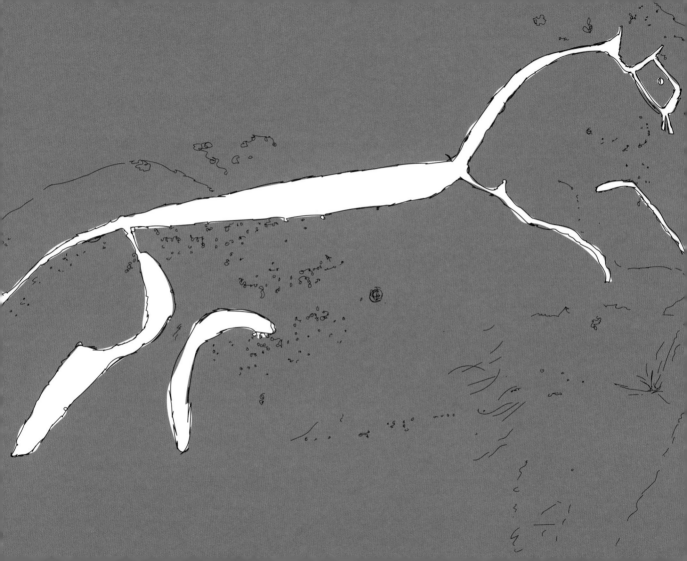

uffington white horse
oxfordshire

There are sixteen white horses cut into chalk landscapes in England. In south-west England, about 19km (12 miles) from Swindon in Wiltshire, lies surely the most impressive – the monumental Bronze Age figure of the Uffington White Horse.

As an artist I have always marvelled at the sheer scale of these beautifully sculpted chalk outline figures, appearing high up on hill ranges and dominating the surrounding landscape. This majestic figure is thought to be over 3,000 years old – the oldest remaining chalk figure in Great Britain.

The horse is 110m (374ft) long and 37m (122ft) tall, and is thought to have some connection to the builders of the nearby Uffington Castle. It is now a Scheduled Ancient Monument.

windsor castle
berkshire

Built in the eleventh century and official residence to Queen Elizabeth II, Windsor Castle in Berkshire is the oldest and largest occupied castle in the world. The entire site covers an area of over 5 hectares (13 acres), with the original castle being a motte and bailey construction, at the centre of which now sits the imposing Round Tower.

The castle is often used by the Queen, who takes up official residence for a month every year from March to April, known as Easter Court. She is also in residence in June for the Order of the Garter chivalric and installation ceremonies and the race meeting at Royal Ascot.

The castle is a very popular tourist attraction, because despite being a royal residence, much of the site is open to the public – including the State Apartments, Queen Mary's famous dolls' house, St George's Chapel, and the Albert Memorial Chapel.

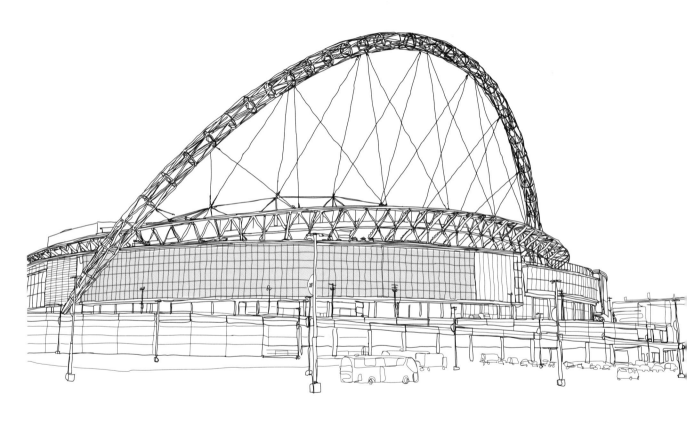

wembley stadium
london

In 1923 Sir Robert McAlpine built a stadium at Wembley in Middlesex for the British Empire Exhibition of 1924. The original plan was to demolish the Empire Stadium following the exhibition, but it was saved and went on to become the famous Wembley Stadium, hosting football matches until its demolition in 2003.

The current Wembley Stadium was opened in 2007. With 90,000 seats, it is the second-largest stadium in Europe (after Camp Nou in Barcelona) and hosts major football matches from FA cup finals to England internationals.

As a proud English football supporter, I miss the iconic twin towers of the original stadium, but this impressive example of modern architecture inspires greatness and will hopefully lead England to the glory we saw in the famous 1966 World Cup.

hampton court palace
surrey

Hampton Court Palace is located on the outskirts of London, in Richmond upon Thames. The palace was originally built for Cardinal Thomas Wolsey in 1514; King Henry VIII took it over in 1528 and it became his favourite palace.

The entire site is over 24 hectares (60 acres) in area, and includes the famous Hampton Court maze (planted in 1690 for King William III of Orange), the Great Vine (the largest grape vine in the world and over 240 years old), and an indoor tennis court for the historic game of real tennis (the racquet sport from which modern tennis is descended).

The palace also has its fair share of legend and ghostly tales. The 'screaming lady' is thought to be the ghost of Catherine Howard, Henry VIII's fifth wife, who was beheaded for treason. The 'grey ghost' of Dame Sybil Penn is also believed to roam the Clock Courts.

buckingham palace
london

In 1761 King George III bought Buckingham House for his wife, Queen Charlotte, initially as a family home – indeed, fourteen of his fifteen children were born there. To this day it remains the London residence of the monarchy and has been the site of many memorable occasions.

Queen Victoria made the house her official residence in 1837, and over the years many major architectural additions have been made. The most recent addition to the palace was the Queen's Gallery, built in 1962 to replace the chapel that was destroyed by a German bomb in the Second World War.

Buckingham Palace houses some of the most beautiful and famous interiors in the country. The State Rooms of the house were opened for public viewing in 1993, but only during August and September while the Queen is not in residence.

battersea power station
london

This wonderful example of modern British design is my favourite building in the world. Designed by Sir Giles Gilbert Scott, who also designed the famous red London telephone box, construction on the power station began in Battersea, south-west London, in 1929.

The building is actually two separate power stations, the first built in the 1930s and the second in the 1950s, and electricity was generated here up until 1983.

Now the site of a major redevelopment, the striking towers remind us of England's rich industrial past and will continue to dominate the London skyline for years to come.

houses of parliament
london

Visitors to London often refer to the Palace of Westminster by its most well-known constituent, Big Ben, although this is actually the name of the main bell in the iconic clock tower, the Elizabeth Tower.

Situated on the banks of the River Thames, in the City of Westminster, the original palace was first constructed in the eleventh century. Fire destroyed the building in the fifteenth and, more savagely, eighteenth centuries and architect Charles Barry was tasked with designing the current building, which was begun in 1840. Only Westminster Hall, which boasts the largest clearspan medieval roof in England, survives from the eleventh century.

Now a Grade I listed building, the palace remains the seat of the United Kingdom government and is also a popular tourist attraction. Big Ben itself (the Great Bell) is over 150 years old and weighs around 14 tonnes (13.7 tons).

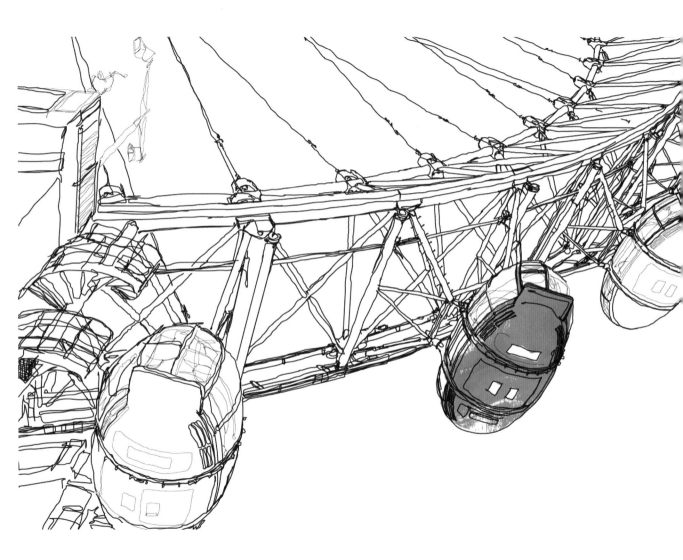

london eye
london

Towering over the South Bank of the River Thames, the London Eye, Europe's largest Ferris wheel, gazes over the capital.

Built to commemorate the millennium in 1999, the Eye stands, amidst some of London's most history-laden sites, as a symbol of modern technology and engineering. It is amazing to behold and both wonderful and difficult to draw!

It is 135m (443ft) high and has a span of 120m (394ft). Each 10-tonne passenger capsule (one for every borough in the capital) can carry 25 people, and the wheel takes roughly half an hour to complete a single revolution.

tower of london

london

A stone's throw from Tower Bridge stands the imposing Tower of London, commissioned in 1066 by William the Conqueror to keep unruly Londoners in check.

The White Tower, which gives the building its name, was commissioned by William in 1078. During its incredible history, the building has served as an armoury, a treasury, a menagerie, the Royal Mint, and a public records office. It is probably best known as the home of the Crown Jewels, which sit in the Jewel House, guarded by armed soldiers.

Now a UNESCO World Heritage Site, the Tower of London is one of England's most popular tourist sites, with 2,894,698 visitors in 2013.

tower bridge
london

Tower Bridge, which crosses London's River Thames, was built in 1894 by over 430 contractors. It spans 244m (801ft) and remains one of London's most recognisable sights, connecting the boroughs of Tower Hamlets and Southwark.

The bridge was constructed with high-level walkways, so that the public could still cross when the bridge was open. These were closed in 1910 due to lack of use.

The bascule bridge opens to a maximum of 86 degrees to allow tall ships to pass along the Thames. In 1952, a London bus driver had to jump the gap when the bridge opened with his bus still on it – aside from minor injuries the driver and passengers miraculously escaped unharmed.

The bridge's now familiar red, white and blue livery was painted in 1977 for the Queen's Silver Jubilee.

the O$_2$
london

To celebrate the turn of the century in 2000, the Millennium Dome was conceived. This unique venue was constructed on the banks of the River Thames in Greenwich, London, to create a memorable spectacle for visitors. Following the opening of the Millennium Experience exhibition on 31 December 1999, it only attracted some 4.5 million visitors throughout 2000 – way below the projected estimate of 12 million.

The Dome quickly became a white elephant, having cost over £700 million to build and spiralling costs thereafter taking the total spend to around £1 billion.

In 2005, the telecomms company O$_2$ sealed a sponsorship deal with the owners and the Dome was officially renamed after the organisation. Since then it has flourished as a major sports and entertainment venue, hosting concerts and events. It was even part of the 2012 London Olympics – gymnastics, basketball and wheelchair basketball events took place in the arena.

The Dome itself is the largest fabric structure in the world, with over 92,900 sq. m (1 million sq. ft) of fabric used in the canopy roof, which is supported by twelve posts. It is 52m (170ft) high and includes a 23,000-seat stadium.

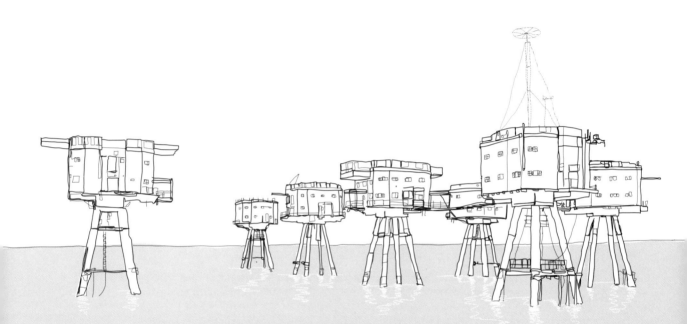

maunsell forts
kent

Several miles off the north Kent coast lie the eerie remains of the Maunsell Forts, a series of fortified towers built to protect the Thames estuary during the Second World War.

Named after Guy Maunsell, the British civil engineer who designed them, the forts consisted of four naval forts known as Fort Roughs Tower, Sunk Head Tower, Tongue Sands, and Knock John. They were sunk into the seabed and became operational in 1942. These were followed in 1943 by three army forts known as Nore, Red Sands and Shivering Sands. These were of a different construction and each fort had seven towers linked by steel catwalks. Many of the 21 original towers have been dismantled, and only thirteen remain.

Abandoned in the 1950s, the forts have been home to pirate radio stations, but are now rusting slowly into the sea. A charity – Project Redsand – is aiming to restore the site on a tower-by-tower basis, and runs occasional trips out to these amazing structures.

chartwell
kent

From 1924, Chartwell was the family home of Sir Winston Churchill right up until his death in 1965, when his wife, Clementine, gave the property to the National Trust.

The house dates back to 1362, taking its name from the chart well found on the property ('chart' being the Kentish name for 'common'). It is also thought that King Henry VIII stayed here while courting the doomed Anne Boleyn in the sixteenth century.

Situated near the Kentish town of Westerham, the house is now preserved as it would have been during Churchill's tenancy, and has been open to the public since 1966.

leeds castle
kent

Originally a Norman stronghold built in 1119, this famous castle lies 8km (5 miles) away from Maidstone in Kent (and not in Leeds, Yorkshire, as I had always assumed as a child!).

Sitting on an island on the River Len, the castle was a royal residence for hundreds of years after being home to Queen Eleanor of Castile, the first wife of King Edward I, who ruled from 1272–1307.

Now a major tourist attraction, Leeds is one of the finest examples of its kind. Lord Conway once described it as 'the loveliest castle in the world'. When you gaze at its magnificent grounds and its picturesque setting, you can understand why.

Over half a million people flock to the castle every year, enjoying its maze, grotto and golf course, as well as, bizarrely, the world's only museum of dog collars.

canterbury cathedral
kent

Canterbury Cathedral in Kent, mother church of the
worldwide Anglican Communion, is seat of the Archbishop
of Canterbury, leader of the Church of England. It is formally
known as the Cathedral and Metropolitical Church of Christ
at Canterbury.

In AD 597 St Augustine, sent by Pope Gregory the Great
as a missionary, established his seat (or *cathedra*) in
Canterbury. Since 1170, when Thomas à Beckett was
famously murdered here, the cathedral has been a special
place of pilgrimage for many. Indeed, as I write, my mother
is completing her own pilgrimage along the Pilgrim's Way,
from Winchester to Canterbury.

white cliffs of dover
kent

The White Cliffs of Dover, which gaze out from Kent across the English Channel towards France, are one of England's most emblematic landmarks.

This stunning coastal feature stretches for about 16km (10 miles) along the south coast, and the sheer cliffs reach over 90m (295ft) in height. The distinctive white colour comes from the chalk of the Kent Downs, and the location has been assigned the status of an Area of Outstanding Natural Beauty.

The cliffs were of huge symbolic value in the Second World War, and are forever immortalized by Vera Lynn's 1942 song '(There'll Be Bluebirds Over) the White Cliffs of Dover'. Many aerial fights took place above the cliffs during the Battle of Britain.

bodiam castle

sussex

Bodiam Castle near Robertsbridge in East Sussex is an archetypal English castle, with its towers, turrets and moat. Built in 1385 by one of King Richard II's knights, the castle passed through many families over the centuries before being dismantled in the seventeenth century.

Bodiam was bought in 1829 by the politician John 'Mad Jack' Fuller, an intriguing local character who was buried sitting in his favourite chair in an 8m (25ft) pyramid in the village of Brightling, a few miles away. The castle was left to the National Trust in the will of Lord Curzon, who owned the site from 1916 and carried out extensive repairs.

Today, the castle is open to the public, with guided walks available as well as seasonal activities for children.

brighton pier

sussex

During the Victorian era, over 100 seaside piers were built in Britain, but sadly only about half remain, many of which are unused. Brighton Pier (originally known as the Palace Pier) in East Sussex is one of the most famous and enduring.

Opened in 1899 and now the most visited pier in the country, Brighton Pier houses fairground rides, a fish and chip restaurant, food stalls and amusement arcades. There is something enduringly inviting about this Victorian structure and it continues to attract hordes of visitors – including my own children, who are always excited to see it, probably due to the traditional seaside fare on offer, such as ice cream, doughnuts and candy floss.

winchester cathedral
winchester

This spectacular Hampshire cathedral is possibly Winchester's most iconic landmark. The Cathedral Church of the Holy Trinity, St Peter, St Paul and St Swithun (to give it its full name) dates from 1079, and is the seat of the Bishop of Winchester and mother church of the diocese of Winchester.

The cathedral boasts Europe's longest nave, and is the burial place of many of England's historical figures, including King Canute and Jane Austen. A beautifully ethereal Antony Gormley sculpture, *Sound II,* is housed in the cathedral's crypt; the crypt occasionally floods, creating an even more mystical and surreal atmosphere.

The cathedral was effectively saved from collapse in 1906 by an extraordinary man, William Walker. A deep-sea diver by trade, William spent six years working underneath the cathedral to lay concrete bags, so that the walls could be underpinned and prevented from sinking into the watery peat foundations.

spinnaker tower
portsmouth

Originally planned to be part of the Millennium Project, this tower in Portsmouth, Hampshire, finally opened in 2005. As a university student in Portsmouth at the time of its conception, I feel a strong affinity towards the tower, not least because it was the design I voted for, along with 60 per cent of the public, who were given three original designs for a public and educational facility to choose from.

Now one of the tallest structures outside London, the Spinnaker Tower reaches 170m (558ft) and provides unparalleled views over Portsmouth Harbour and across the Solent. Due to its construction, the tower is able to flex up to 15cm (6in) in high winds. There are three viewing decks, the first of which includes the Sky Walk glass floor, the largest in Europe. The second has a café. The top deck, the Crow's Nest, allows visitors to admire the view from 110m (360ft) and is open to the elements.

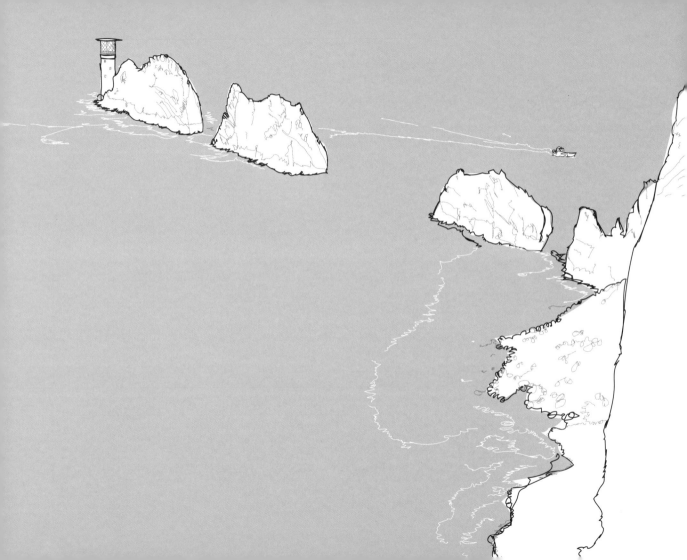

the needles

isle of wight

On the south coast of England, this collection of three chalk stacks off the coast of the Isle of Wight is one of the most well-known rock formations in the world.

The name of the feature actually comes from the missing fourth stack, which stood in the gap you can clearly see. This stack was known as Lot's Wife, and was shaped like a needle. In 1764, when the 36m (118ft) needle fell into the sea during a storm, the impact was felt as far away as Portsmouth.

On the far end of the rocks is the Needles lighthouse, which is 33m (108ft) tall. It was built in 1859 and the last lighthouse keepers left in 1994 when it became fully automated.

Today tourists can admire amazing views from the cliff tops, from a boat or nearby cable car at Alum Bay; there are also many local attractions, including the Needles Old Battery and New Battery, looked after by the National Trust.

brownsea island
dorset

Sitting in the stunning location of Poole Harbour in Dorset, this small island is famous for being one of the few places in England where you can see wild red squirrels, and also as being the first camp of the Scout movement in 1907.

The island is only 2.4km (1½ miles) long and 1.2km (¾ mile) wide, yet it has a long and varied history, beginning as early as the fifth century. In the ninth century, a small chapel was built on the island by the monks of nearby Cerne Abbey. Henry VIII took over the island following the dissolution of the monasteries, and the first castle was built in 1547.

It was thought the island was once used to harbour famous pirates, and over the years it changed owners several times, including William Benson who, in 1707, transformed the castle from a stronghold into a residence. Brownsea Island is now owned by the National Trust.

corfe castle
dorset

The spectacular ruins of Corfe Castle tower above the local countryside on the Isle of Purbeck (actually a peninsula) in Dorset. William the Conqueror built the castle in the eleventh century, and it was one of the earliest stone castles in England.

Once used to house the Crown Jewels, the castle fell out of royal ownership and was acquired by staunch Royalists, the Bankes family. When Civil War broke out, the formidable Lady Mary Bankes and a garrison of just 80 soldiers saw off a six-week siege. Despite many daring attempts to rescue 'Brave Dame Mary' she refused to leave her home, but was eventually forced to surrender and the Parliamentarians reduced the castle to the ruin we see today. However, Lady Mary kept the seals and keys of the castle in recognition of her courage – and she lived to see her estate returned and the restoration of the monarchy in 1660.

Today, Corfe Castle is run by the National Trust, who open it all year round. It remains a romantic ruin as many of the stones pulled down by the Parliamentarians were recycled by locals to build their own homes.

salisbury cathedral
salisbury

I first visited Salisbury Cathedral in Wiltshire (formally
known as the Cathedral Church of the Blessed Virgin Mary)
as a young child, and was immediately in awe of its sheer
scale and magnificence.

The main body of the cathedral was completed in 1258, and
later additions include the spire and the cloisters, both of
which hold records for their size – the tallest and largest in
England respectively.

Visitors can also view one of the few remaining copies
of the Magna Carta and the world's oldest working clock.

stonehenge
wiltshire

As a child, I remember seeing Stonehenge from the nearby road and being amazed by the majesty of this ancient site, about 13km (8 miles) from Salisbury in Wiltshire. It is one of a number of Neolithic and Bronze Age monuments in the area.

The site has much mystery and intrigue attached to it. It is thought to be over 5,000 years old, and in 1986 it was designated a World Heritage Site. Its history encompasses a cremation cemetery, and it is generally thought that the stones, aligned with the movements of the sun, form a prehistoric temple.

While the smaller Sarsen Stones came from the Marlborough Downs, some 40km (25 miles) north of Stonehenge, the huge inner bluestones came from the Preseli Mountains in south Wales. The logistics are almost unthinkable when you realize that they weigh up to 4 tonnes each.

The stones are managed by English Heritage, and attract over a million visitors every year. The occasion of the summer solstice is a big draw, when thousands gather to see the sun rise on the longest day of the year; the winter solstice, too, attracts a crowd.

bath's roman baths

bath

The spa city of Bath in Somerset houses the only hot springs in Britain, one of the wonders of Roman Britain. This well-preserved monument is now housed inside nineteenth-century buildings, and the baths themselves remain below street level.

The baths contain water that has been heated by geothermal energy and forced up though limestone faults. The temperature reaches 46°C (114.8°F), although the water has cooled slightly to 36°C (96.8°F) by the time it reaches the Great Bath. Perfect bathing temperature!

The Great Bath was fed by what was known as the Sacred Spring, and is 1.6m (5ft 3in) deep with steps on all sides for easy access. The bath once stood inside a magnificent vaulted hall.

Visitors can also see the other areas of this amazing complex, including the Temple, courtyard, changing rooms, saunas and other smaller plunge pools. There is also a superb museum and restaurant, the Pump Room, on site.

stourhead

wiltshire

Stourhead is a large estate near Mere in Wiltshire. It consists of a stunning Palladian mansion, the village of Stourton, world-famous landscape gardens, farmland and woodland.

The estate was owned by the Stourton family for over 500 years. When it was sold to Henry Hoare I in 1717, he pulled down the old manor house and built the Palladian mansion in 1721. Stourhead was made over to National Trust in 1946, although Hoare's descendants remained on the estate until 1956 and an apartment is still retained for family residence.

A dam was built to create the artificial lake, around which sit temples, Gothic buildings and rare flora. The grounds were much admired in the eighteenth century, being described as 'a living work of art'. They earned Henry Hoare II, who inherited the estate in 1725 and ran it until he died in 1785, the name 'Henry the Magnificent'. Today the gardens continue to flourish, and visitors come to walk and enjoy the beautiful 1,072-hectare (2,650-acre) site through the seasons.

cheddar gorge
somerset

This dramatic landscape in the Mendip Hills in Somerset, an Area of Outstanding Natural Beauty, is the biggest gorge in Britain. It stretches for over 5km (3 miles), dropping some 137m (450ft) into the hillside. The north side of the gorge is owned by the National Trust.

Formed by melting permafrost, the gorge contains a network of stunning caves created by underwater flooding. Two of the largest caves, Gough's Cave and Cox's Cave, are open to the public. Gough's Cave was discovered in 1903 and contained the skeleton of the 9,000-year-old Cheddar Man, along with other important artefacts.

The visitor centre at Cheddar provides tourists with a wealth of information and activities. The area itself is visited by over half a million people every year, who flock to admire the incredible views and step into England's prehistoric past.

clifton suspension bridge
bristol

The graceful structure straddling the Avon Gorge to join Bristol and North Somerset is the Clifton Suspension Bridge. Designed by Isambard Kingdom Brunel, the bridge is 412m (1,352ft) long and officially opened in 1864, some five years after Brunel's death. This was predominately due to the fact that the project had been plagued by financial and contractual issues.

The bridge was originally designed to carry horse-drawn traffic and pedestrians, but such was Brunel's brilliance that the bridge is capable of carrying nearly 9,000 modern vehicles per day.

There are many local stories connected to the bridge, not least the tale of Sarah Ann Henley, a local barmaid, who in 1885 threw herself from the bridge following a split from her lover. As she plunged the 75m (246ft) to the bottom of the gorge, it is thought that her large crinoline skirt slowed her descent, and she landed injured but alive in the mud. She went on to live into her eighties.

greenway
devon

Proclaimed by Agatha Christie to be 'the loveliest place in the world', Greenway is a stunning house looking out over the River Dart, near Brixham in Devon.

The site has been in existence since the 1490s, but little is known of its origins. A Tudor house was built here by the Gilbert family in the sixteenth century, but the house is now well known for its association with the best-selling novelist Agatha Christie, who bought the house in 1938 and used it as a holiday home until her death in 1976. The house became home to her daughter, Rosalind, and was later opened by the National Trust in 2000.

Greenway is now open to the public, who can explore the walled gardens and discover the Ralegh's Boathouse (the scene of Marlene Tucker's death in Christie's *Dead Man's Folly*). There are also many events taking place in the grounds, from an outdoor cinema to children's adventure days.

the eden project
cornwall

Opened in 2001, the Eden Project is a series of huge, greenhouse-type structures known as biomes, situated in an old china quarry just outside St Blazey in Cornwall. It is the brainchild of Tim Smit (who had earlier restored the Lost Gardens of Heligan), and the complex was designed to house some of the world's most amazing and significant plants.

Work began in 1998 and people flocked through the doors when the site opened in March 2001. There are two main areas to visit. The Tropical Biome houses species such as coffee, banana and rubber trees, while the Mediterranean Biome contains plants such as olives and grapevines.

The Eden Project is not only a wonderful way to see hundreds of plant species and amazing sculptures, but also provides extensive ecological education. The site itself uses green energy and recycled water.

st michael's mount
cornwall

This small, picturesque island lies off the southern coast of
Cornwall, and is connected to the small town of Marazion by
a man-made causeway. At low tide, you can walk across to the
island. St Michael, who in Cornish legend appeared to fishermen
here in AD 495, gives the island its name.

The island was once a key part of Cornwall's booming tin-mining
industry, and has been a centre of religious significance as well
as a site of many key battles throughout the ages.

The Mount is steeped in local folklore, and was said to have
been built by a giant called Cormoran. According to legend, the
giant was felled by a local boy named Jack, who tricked him into
falling into a deep pit, where a well now stands. This success
earned him the title of Jack the Giant Killer.

Owned by the St Aubyn family since the seventeenth century,
the National Trust opened the island to visitors in the 1960s.

cornish mines & engines

The county of Cornwall is dotted with reminders of its mining past, and ruins of long-closed engine houses can be seen on much of today's landscape.

It is thought that the tin ore cassiterite was mined in Cornwall as long ago as the Bronze Age. In the early nineteenth century, this became a major industry in the area, with about 600 steam engines working to mine the precious metal. This brought great employment and wealth for a long period. Towards the end of the century, mining was in decline, and the skilled workers left for more profitable areas.

Myth and legend also surround the mines. The wonderfully named Ding Dong Mine, one of Cornwall's oldest, is said to have been visited by Joseph of Arimathea – as he was a tin trader. Legend also has it that a young Jesus visited and addressed the miners.

tintagel
cornwall

Tintagel is one of England's most mysterious and enigmatic sites. Forever associated with Arthurian legend, the village and castle located on the north coast of Cornwall are shrouded in mystery and legend. In the twelfth century, Tintagel was mentioned in a book by Geoffrey of Monmouth as being the site of King Arthur's conception.

In 1233 Richard of Cornwall built a castle on the headland; this later succumbed to disrepair and the elements, and was left as a ruin for many years. When interest in the Arthurian legend was reawakened by the Victorians, Tintagel became the focus of tourists. Local sites such Merlin's Cave and King Arthur's Footprint have added to the mystery.

There are many other attractions in Tintagel, such as the medieval hall house that was once, among other things, a Victorian post office (now refurbished by the National Trust), as well as stunning beaches, caves and countryside.

acknowledgements

The author would like to thank: Ian Hale,
Emyr Jones, Ethan Tucker, David Warwick,
Kol Tregaskes, Dawn Wigley, Danny Simpson,
Nathan Rupert, Sarah Dawson, Andy Spencer,
Jeremy Gillies, Steven Butler, Craig Olivant,
Jason Wells, Xavier de Jauréguiberry,
Mark Vanstone, Paul Murray, J. Learmonth,
Dave Price, Tommy McMillan, Robert Scarth,
Mick's Flicks, Jon Barbour, Carol Henson,
Howard Scott and Katy Harmer.